My Story

A Year in the Life of a Country Girl

by Ida Burnett
age 15

January 1, 1880 - December 31, 1880

Logan, New York
Schuyler County

New York History Review Press
Elmira, New York

My Story - A Year in the Life of a Country Girl
by Ida Burnett, 1880
transcribed by Diane Janowski

Published by New York History Review Press
Elmira, New York

Copyright © 2009 Diane Janowski.
Notice of Rights. All rights reserved. No part of this book may be reproduced or transmitted in any form by any means, electronic, mechanical, photocopying, recording or otherwise, without the prior written permission of the author. For more information on getting permission for reprints and excerpts, contact us through our website.
www.NewYorkHistoryReview.com

This book was designed and laid out in Adobe InDesign using typeface Adobe Garamond Pro.

For the latest on New York History Review, please visit
www.NewYorkHistoryReview.com

ISBN: 978-0-578-03072-2

First Edition
Printed in the United States of America

for Mate

Ida's diary in its current condition. Courtesy of the Eleanor Barnes Library, Elmira, New York.

Table of Contents

Foreward..8

Map of Logan, New York......................................10

People in this Diary...11

My Story - A Country Girl's Diary............................15

Bibiliography..74

What happened to them?....................................75

Afterward..76

Foreward

In our *Learning from History* series of Upstate New York diaries, accounts of young people's lives on the farm, or in the home, help us to understand their thoughts and experiences. Each narrative offers a unique perspective on teenage life in rural New York, and serves as an important primary resource in the study of American history.

My Story - A Year in the Life of a Country Girl is the journal of 15-year-old Ida Burnett of Logan, New York - about 3½ miles from downtown Hector. Ida was born in 1865. She was the daughter of Henry and Esther Burnett. The 1870 New York census lists the family in Phelps, New York. They later moved to Red Hook, New York where the last two children were born, and then finally to the Mathews Road in Logan, New York.

Beginning on January 1, 1880, Ida recorded the events of her life in a small 3¼ x 6 inch pocket diary with three entries to the page in nice handwriting. Her notations were confined to the spaces allotted and are written in pencil or ink. Her handwriting is mostly legible, except for a few names or places that cannot be deciphered. The photographed pages from her diary are actual size. Ida's spelling is left as she spelled it. Clarifications have been added in brackets.

Ida lived with her parents, two sisters, and three brothers at home (an older brother and sister lived nearby). Ida was generally very happy in her life – she enjoyed her family, friends, parties, and boyfriends. She attended school semi-regularly. Going to school was not as important to her as doing household work and farm chores. She was a very hard worker at home. For several months of the diary, Ida worked for a family in North Hector, New York (now the town of Valois). She hated it and was terribly homesick. In the whole year of her diary, she did not not venture more than twenty miles from her home.

My Story - A Year in the Life of a Country Girl invites us into the daily life of an upstate New York teenager, through her own words and experiences. We hear Ida's voice as she shares her joys, sorrows, and enthusiasm for life in a rural farming community.

The Eleanor Barnes Library acquired Ida Burnett's diary in 2008. So far as is known, this transcription is its first published version.

Diane Janowski, Publisher
New York History Review

Ida Burnett's family lived on Mathews Road, about ¾ mile from Logan, New York. Photograph by Allen C. Smith, 2008.

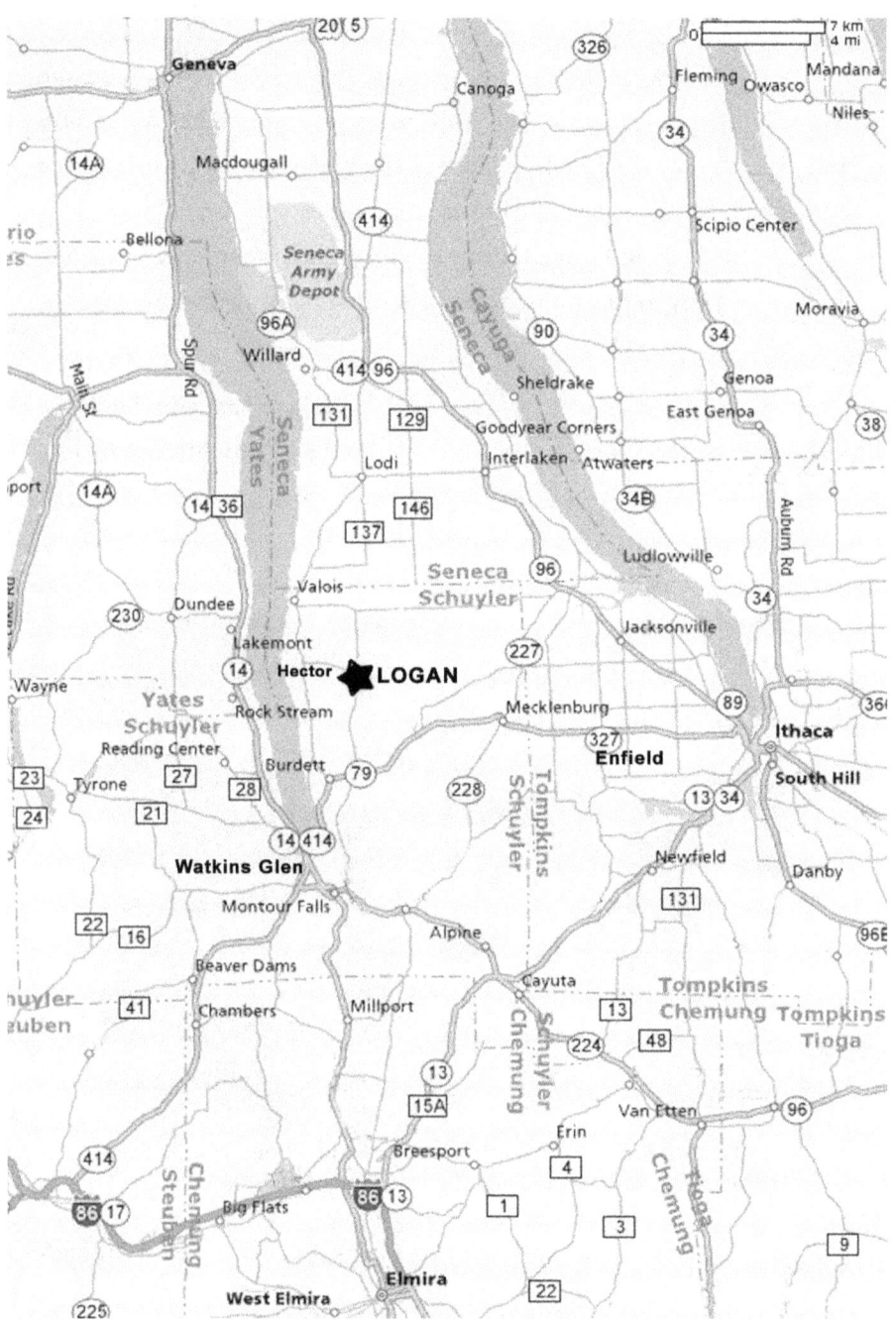

Logan, New York and surroundings. Logan is 9 miles from Watkins Glen, and 25 miles from Ithaca.

People in this Diary

Ida's family in 1880

Pa – Henry, age 53, farmer
Ma – Esther, age 45
Mate Stilwell [Mary Stilwell] - Ida's oldest sister, age 24
Frank Stilwell [Stillwell] - Mate's husband, farm laborer, age 28
Henry - brother, age 20
Carrie - sister, age 17
Ada - sister, age 13
Wallace - brother, age 11
Earnest or Ernest - brother, age 7
Frank - brother, age 4

Friends and Neighbors

Charlie Andrews - age 38, book seller
Lulu Andrews - age 14, daughter of Charlie
George Baker - age 18, lived in Enfield, New York
Mary Baker - age 13, lived in Enfield, New York
Will Ballard - age 22, farm laborer
John Bell - age 65, farmer
Ida Bell - age 23, school teacher
George Bohn [Boyd?]
Mrs. Bond [Lottie] - age 39, nearby neighbor
Anna Boyes - [Boyce?]
Henry Boyd - age 23
Dr. Briggs
Pary Brown [Perry] - age 16, farm laborer
Frank Chandler - age 21, domestic servant
Charlie [Charley Saterly/Satterly?]
C. J. Compton
Ezekell Compton
Arthur Connolly - age 20, farm laborer, nearby neighbor

Jonnie [John] Couse - age 18, nearby neighbor
Joseph Couse - age 12, nearby neighbor
Dave [David] Devit
Niles Devit
Billey [William] Dickerson - age 34, fruit grower
Emma Dickerson - age 20, a teacher
Mary Dickerson - age 19, a teacher
Monroe Dickenson
Henry Dickenson - Ida's dinner date
Alex Dunham - age 38, farmer
Irving Dunham - age 12, son of Alex
Ed Ely - age 17, fixed-up boyfriend for Ida
Elmer [Mathews] - age 18, nearby neighbor
Fannie [Rogers] - age 16
Fred [Case] - age 17, nearby neighbor
George - Carrie's boyfriend
Mate Gittens - [Mary or May] - age 24, Hector
Charlie Hager - age 23, store clerk in North Hector
Ida Howell - age 15, daughter of Robert
Robert Howell - age 55, farmer
Hugh - a fine boy
Jessie
Cara Jonson
Orvil Jonson
Katie [Tailor or Taylor]
Manroe Kingsley [Monroe] - age 32, carpenter
Will Husten - age 8, nearby neighbor
Mrs. Loose [Emma Luce] - age 43, housekeeper
Jasson Loose [Jason Luce] - age 22, farm laborer, worked for Alex
    Dunham, maybe son of Emma
Minnie Loose [Luce] - age 13, daughter of Emma
Parson Loose [Luce]
Mr. Malone
Marian
Ezekel Mathews - nearby neighbor
Manerva Mathews - nearby neighbor
Elmer Mathews - age 18, nearby neighbor

Marion Mathews - age 16, nearby neighbor
Charlie Matison [Mattison] - age 12
Carrie Mekutchen [McCuahern] - age 16
Mr. [Abram] Mekeel - age 50, New York State Assemblyman
    from 1878-79 and a farmer, lived next to Mate Stillwell
Mrs. [Jane] Mekeel - age 48
Carrie Mekeel - daughter of the Mekeels
Will McNetten - age 10
Dan Molton
Irvin Moore - age 22, farmer,
Pid - Peter Stillwell ?
Pery [Pary, Perry Brown]
Fannie [Rogers] - age 16
Mrs. Rich – lived in Logan
Em [Emily] Rudy - age 13, nearby neighbor
Will [Willes] Rudy - age 17, nearby neighbor
Fred Rudy nearby neighbor
Mrs. Sacket
Hattie Seybolt - age 12
Stephen Seybolt
Whitley Smith
Isaiah Strater [Strader]
Avery Thomas
Poly [Polly VanWarmer or VanWormer] - age 36, dressmaker
Sattie Van Wormer
Eva Weaver
Jane Weaver
Bob Yates
Zeek - maybe Ezekell Compton or Ezekel Mathews

JANUARY, THURSDAY 1. 1880.

I and Ma got breakfast. Miss Vandoren has been here all day. and Mate and Frank has been here all the afternoon. Alex Bingham and A. Brom Wyatt is here.

FRIDAY 2.

I went to school to day. Corrie went up to Mates this afternoon. and Fred Baker was here. Monroe King Sleyzer was here to dinner. Jane called this evening.

SATURDAY 3.

I and Ma got breakfast went to school. Pa went to Reynoldsville. Mate was here all day. We had company in the evening. six Baker children was here and the Pickens. we did not go to bed till two o'clock.

My Story

by Ida Burnett, Logan, New York 1880

January, Thursday 1. 1880.
I and Ma got breakfast. Miss Vandoren has been here all day and Mate and Frank has been here all the afternoon. Alex Dunham and Abram Wyatt is here.

January, Friday 2. 1880.
I went to school today. Carrie went up to Mate's this afternoon and Fred Baker was here. Manroe [Monroe] Kingsley was here to dinner. Jane called this evening.

January, Saturday 3. 1880.
I and Ma got breakfast. Pa went to Reynoldsville. Mate was here all day. We had company in the evening – six Baker children was here and three Dickens. We did not go to bed until two o'clock.

January, Sunday 4. 1880.
We did not get up very early this morning - ate breakfast at ten. Did not go to church this morning. Pa went to Trumansburg today - nor to church tonight. Carrie looked for George a little tonite but he did not come. It reigned [rained].

January, Monday 5. 1880.
Ma got breakfast this morning alone. I stayed to-home from school and washed. Ed went to milk. Mate Gittens wiped the breakfast and dinner dishes for Ma.

January, Tuesday 6. 1880.
I went to school today. Charlie Matison left the school I ----we're going to Rudy's and stay all night. I ironed my dress.

January, Wednesday 7. 1880.
Ma got the moste of the breakfast. I baked the pancakes. Went to school today. Mate was down here all day and took the boyes [boys'] shirts home with her to make.

January, Thursday 8. 1880.
I went home with Em [Emily] Rudy last night – we had a splendid time. I whispered in school today and the teacher made me write a word 100 times for it and I am a-doing it now.

January, Friday 9. 1880.
I and Ma got breakfast. Went to school. Mate has been here all day. Ma and her went to Bardett [Burdett]. Ma got I and Carrie a black cashmere dress. They both cost $23.90. Mine cost alone $16.90. I was down to Jane's a little while. Went over [to] the lake to see her sister.

January, Saturday 10. 1880.
I got breakfast. I and Ada washed the dishes. I and Ma went to meeting. Carrie did not get up until 8 o'clock. Poly worked a half a day on our dresses. Carrie went home with Poly. Mate Gittens, Will, and the babies is here.

January, Sunday 11. 1880.
I got breakfast and washed the dishes. I and Ma went to meeting. Carrie come home with us. Carrie got a letter from George yesterday. Answered it today. Saw the two birds. [Ida mentions her pet bird later in the diary.] Elmer helped me get the horses this morning. We went to meeting tonight.

January, Monday 12. 1880.
Henry and Pa went to Seneca Falls, Geneva, and Canandaigua. Carrie washed and I done the housework. I did not go to school today. Ed went after the children. Mate has been down all day. Ed went after the school children. I got all ready to go after Poly - but did not go. Will and the family got back to knight.

went over the lake to see her
sister

JANUARY, SATURDAY 10. 1880.

I got breakfast and Ma
washed the dishes. Carrie did
not get up until 8 oclock
Pop worked a half of a day
on his dress. Carrie went
home with Pop. Mate com
down in the after noon. Mate
& Tens & Will and the babies

SUNDAY 11.

I got breakfast and wash
ed the dishes I and ma
Went to meeting Carrie came
home with us Carrie got
a letter from George yes
terday answered it today
saw the two brides Marie
Elmer helped me get the
horses this morning

MONDAY 12.

we went to school today
henry and he went to wilkins
to day he went to Seneca fall
geneva and Canandaigua.
Carrie washed and I done the house
work I did not go to school to
day Ed went after the children
Kate has been down all day
Ed went after the school children
I got all ready to go to Kay Bs but
did not go to Will and Chy

January, Tuesday 13. 1880.
I went down after Poly - stoped to the grosey [grocery] and the minister was there. I did not go to school today. Poly fitted my dress. Did not go the ladies aid society tonite. Carrie done all of the work today and I am to do it tomorrow.

January, Wednesday 14. 1880.
Carrie slept with Poly last night. I have done all of the work today. Rote a letter to Charlie Salisbury today for Wallace. George Weaver was here this evening. Henry went a-hunting. Poly has been here all day to sew. Pa went to Watkins – got my shoes – they cost 85¢.

January, Thursday 15. 1880.
I did not go to school. Poly has worked on our dresses. Pa went to Watkins. Stephen Seybolt and Parson Loose [Luce] was here today. Mate was down a little while at night. Will Husten and Billey Dickerson called.

January, Friday 16. 1880.
We did not get up very early this morning. Poly worked all day and got done tonight. Henry went and took her home. Ed went to Shelling [?]. I have got an awful pain in my side tonight. Had some chickens for dinner. Going to Enfield tomorrow.

January, Saturday 17. 1880.
Manerva Mathews was down here all day. Mate Gittens went to Logan a-foot and got the news. I went and met her. She read *Little Brownie* to me. I got dinner. Carrie washed dishes.

January, Sunday 18. 1880.
We did not go to church this morning but we did tonight. Mrs. Smith and her children rode over with us. Mrs. Socket [Sacket] was over tonight. There was a man here yesterday and invited us to a surprise party for Monroe Dickenson.

January, Monday 19. 1880.
I went to school today and traded seats with Henry and Will and am sick of my boredom a-ready. Carrie washed. Wallace is sick tonight. I went to Jane's and bought some butter.

January, Tuesday 20. 1880.
I did not get up till breakfast was ready. Went to school. Emily Rudy came home with us tonight and stayed all knight. I and Em and Ada slept in the parler bedroom and we had to get up and make the bed a half dozen times.

January, Wednesday 21. 1880.
I went to school today. Ada went home with Em Rudy and stayed all night. Ed went to the Library but did not any of the rest of us go. He got the paper and I and Carrie up and went up stairs and Mate Gittens red *Little Brownie* to us.

January, Thursday 22. 1880.
I went to school today. We practiced our pieces for tomorrow. The boys got to fooling and Henry got mad at John Bell and Will Rudy tore the seat of Henry's pants awful. He had a notion to come home but he did not.

January, Friday 23. 1880.
I went to school. We spoke pieces in the afternoon. We ---- over ---- about *Aunt Peggie's Courtship*. I was "Aunt Peggie." I went to a surprise party tonight to Manroe Dickenson. Henry Dickenson took me to supper. Carrie went with George.

January, Saturday 24. 1880.
I washed the breakfast dishes. Got dinner and washed them dishes. Frank and Mate came down. Mate and Frank went down to Mrs. Bond's this afternoon. I moped [mopped]. Ada sowed on her quilt all day. Ed took quite a shine to Mary Baker tonight and she is the best girl that I ever seen.

January, Sunday 25. 1880.
Ada got breakfast. Ma and Carrie washed the dishes. We got all ready to church this morning, but we did not go – it got so late – but we went in the evening. Mate Gittens and Jane Weaver went with us.

January, Monday 26. 1880.
I went to school today. Carrie and Frankie went to Logan and got the

male. She got a letter from George. She was very glad to hear from him. Mr. Mowel was buried today. I went to sleep twice in school today. Carrie washed.

January, Tuesday 27. 1880.
I went to school – and it reigned [rained] all day but we went to a ----- party up to Ezekel Mathews just the same. We had a splended time. We got home about 2 o'clock. Henry waited on Marian like a gentleman.

January, Wednesday 28. 1880.
I went to school. Will Rudy came home with me to stay all night. There is a spelling school to Logan tonight but I did not go. Henry, Will, Ed, and Wallace has gon and I am a-waiting for them to fetch the male. Mate is here now.

January, Thursday 29. 1880.
I went to school. Henry and Stephen Seybolt went a-hunting. Will took his dinner but did not eat it. I was 10 [?] tonight. Pa went to Watkins [Watkins Glen, NY] and Havana. Did not get home very early. Ed went to ----- to get his *Democrat* [probably the Rochester *Democrat & Chronicle*] to go to Enfield Center.

January, Friday 30. 1880.
I went to school. The teacher examined all of the schoolars. I didn't pass any, but I came pretty near in everything, but a miss is as good as a mile. Carrie washed the ruffles in my dress and put them back in.

January, Saturday 31. 1880.
We went to Enfield today and when we was a-getting ready, Will, Rich and Stephen Seybolt came over and wanted Henry to go downtown with them. We did not go to bed till 8 o'clock Sunday morning.

February, Sunday 1. 1880.
We all went to church. I am to Enfield now. I went with Fred, Carrie went with George. We broke the wagon this morning. Fred and I went in the buggy tonight. We went and took a ride after meeting – ate supper after we got home.

February, Monday 2. 1880.
I am to Baker's yet and have had a splended time. We came home today, kissed all of the folks goodbye. Fred is the greatest boy that I ever saw. When we got to Dickinson's we stoped and got our supper. It was 7 o'clock when we got home. Earnest is seven years old today.

February, Tuesday 3. 1880.
Pa is to Watkins a--------. I did not go to school today. They wanted I should stay the rest of the day. Henry and Mary Dickenson went to Baker's with us. Ada went with Frank and Mate. It snows offul today. The snow is two feet deep.

February, Wednesday 4. 1880.
They did not [let] any of us go to school today. Frank and Mate is here. Carrie washed. We all went to Logan at night. Pa has been to Watkins all of the weak.

February, Thursday 5. 1880.
I went to school. Mate went from here over to Stilwells. Pa come home tonight and brang an organ with him, but he hain't bought it yet. We got the paper last night. Henry went a-hunting and Frank went with him.

February, Friday 6. 1880.
I went to school a-foot. Frank Stilwell and Pid are here. Henry took Pid to Watkins and got him a ring. Jane and Eva and Allie were up here last night. Pa came home tonight at twelve o'clock.

February, Saturday 7. 1880.
I made some bread and pies. Mooped [mopped] the floor, got the dinner, washed them dishes. Carrie has got the belleyache and she has done the ironing. Ada has sewed on her quilt all day. Ma hain't very well.

February, Sunday 8. 1880.
I got breakfast this morning. We all went to church in the morning and at night. Carrie went home with the minister. Jasson Loose [Jason Luce]

FEBRUARY THURSDAY 12 1880

I got breakfast. I did not go to school. I and Ma washed. Carrie is on the house work. I drove up to the lecture and got the paper. Fred of Barn was here and hired out he is coming to work Monday.

FRIDAY 13

I did not go to school Carrie is better. We got all ready to go to Bob Noteses to a surprise party but it rained so we stayed at home. Carrie odd ? feels awful bad about it.

SATURDAY 14

I got breakfast. Mob and Frank has been to town all day. Jason Corse is here I helped Ada on her quilt all day what time I got. Mite Gillins has got the both ake. Will Rudy is to work here yet.

come home with us. Henry Dickenson was to Zeek's. Orvil Jonson and Emma Dickerson was to meeting together tonight.

February, Monday 9. 1880.
I went to school. Henry got an invitation to a surprise party at Bob Yates's next Friday night. Pa bought the Orgon today. Frank and Mate are here and are a-going to stay all night. Will Rudy come home from school with us.

February, Tuesday 10. 1880.
I got a letter from Anna Boyes last Saturday and sent the answer today. I did not go to school. I baked a cake to take to the nite party but did not go. Henry got a letter from George. Mary Baker says that if Henry will write to her – that she will answer it.

February, Wednesday 11. 1880.
Carrie is sick. I got breakfast. There is a spelling school to Logan tonight – they didn't anybody go but Ed. We sent by him for the teacher but he did not think of it. I did not go to school. I and Ada don all of the work.

February, Thursday 12. 1880.
I got breakfast. Did not go to school. I and Ada washed. Carrie don the housework. Ed went to the lecture and got the paper. Fred Bun [Bunn] was here and hired out. He is coming to work on Monday.

February, Friday 13. 1880.
I did not go to school. Carrie better. We got all ready to go to Bob Yates's to a surprise party, but it rained [so] we stayed at home. Carrie and Ed feals awful bad about it.

February, Saturday 14. 1880.
I got breakfast. Mate and Frank has been down all day. Jason Loose is here. I helped Ada on her quilt all day – what time I got. Mate Gittens has got the toothache. Will Rudy is to work here yet.

February, Sunday 15. 1880.
I got breakfast. Ma is very sick. Pa went down to Dr. Brigg's and got some medicine for her. I and Carrie got each other a valentine last night. We thought that mine come from Charlie ---- and [Carrie's] from George. I rote to Charlie and Carrie to George.

February, Monday 16. 1880.
I and Ada got breakfast. Ma is a little better. I did not go to school. Earnest and Wallace went and the teacher came home with them to stay all night. Jane is here. S--- came to work but Fred did not. Will come back this morning.

February, Tuesday 17. 1880.
The teacher stayed all nite last night. I did not go to school. Pa went to Dr. Briggs's and got some medicine for Ma and Carrie and he said that she must not do a lot of work. Jane was here. Ma hain't any better.

February, Wednesday 18. 1880.
I did not go to school. I baked bread and Ada ironed most of the clows [clothes]. I was up today. We was awful tired at night. Ed went to Smith's. Jonnie Couse was here.

February, Thursday 19. 1880.
I went to Jones's and bought a dozen eggs. I was up today. Mrs. Bond was up a little while. We got a letter from Mr. VanWinkle.

February, Friday 20. 1880
I did not go to school. Ma was worse and Henry went after the doctor. Mate and Frank is here. Mate Gittens has helped us all day. Jane was here. Mrs. Smith was here a little while.

February, Saturday 21. 1880.
We expected the teacher and her brother down last nite but they did not come. Mate and Frank was down. Pa and Henry and Wallace went to Watkins. Wallace and Ada went down to Brownes.

February, Sunday 22. 1880.
Wallace took Hattie Seybold to supper and Pery took Ada. I did not go to meeting in the morning. George Bohn [?] was here and went to meeting with us at night. Fred came after him about fore o'clock.

February, Monday 23. 1880.
I got breakfast very early. I have to keep all of Pa's accounts now [that] Ma is sick. Pa went to Logan too times today. Frank Chandler came pretty near coming with us but stayed awhile. Henry got an invite to a surprise party.

February, Tuesday 24, 1880
I and Henry got breakfast. Henry and Will Rudy went a-hunting. There is a nite party down to Robert Howell's tonight but did not any of us go. Henry was so tired. Pa discharged Will R. this morning. I washed.

February, Wednesday 25. 1880.
Pa is mad and got the moste of the breakfast. Henry says that he is a-going a-visiting tonite and he gets over it and did not get back tonite. Pa discharged Will and Ed today. Mrs. Loose and Minnie [are here]. Mate and Frank are here.

February, Thursday 26. 1880.
Mrs. [Loose] and Minnie stayed all nite. She helped me iron this forenoon. Got mad at Minnie and sent her home. Carrie went and took Mrs. Loose home and went to the minister's. Mrs. Seybolt, Mrs. Bond, and ------------ is here.

February, Friday 27. 1880.
Henry hain't got back yet. Pa went to Havana yesterday. Mate and Will [Gittens] are a-packing up to go tomorrow. I got breakfast and we all squalled because Henry don't come home.

February, Saturday 28. 1880.
I got breakfast. Mate and Will is gone. Henry has got home. Jason

came home with him and stayed all nite. Ma red to us all of the evening. We all was glad to see Henry.

February, Sunday 29. 1880.
Ada got breakfast. Jason went home before breakfast. We did not go to meeting in the morning nor at night. Jason came over. We all rote invites for a surprise party.

March, Monday 1. 1880.
I got breakfast and washed all day. Joseph Couse was here a little while. Pa went to Logan. Mr. Van Doren was here and told us that Carrie [the school teacher] was to sicke to teach and there hain't a-gon to be any more school.

March, Tuesday 2. 1880.
I got breakfast. I and Ada went down to Bond's a-visiting and Will Gittens was there. When we got home Carrie had supper ready and Frank Stilwell was here.

March, Wednesday 3. 1880.
I and [Ada] got breakfast. I intended to go to Mrs. Tracie's [Tracy's] but did not. I got two letters from Enfield Center. One was from Mary Baker and the other was from Charlie. I was glad to here from them.

March, Thursday 4. 1880.
Ada helped me get breakfast again. I was to Jones's a [few] minutes this morning. Mate and Frank was here. --- VanWormer is here. Ada, Hattie, Mattie, and Flore [Florence] Bond went for a horse back ride.

March, Friday 5. 1880.
I got breakfast alone. Set my table last night. I got a letter from Ann Koyes and answered Mary Baker today. I rote lots to her. Frank Stilwell is here again. Pa went to Logan tonight.

March, Saturday 6. 1880.
Ada got breakfast and done the ironing and went up to C----'s a-visit-

ing. I am 15 years old today. Will Rudy is here to work today. Jason Loose commenced work here last Thursday.

March, Sunday 7. 1880.
Pa is 53 years old today. We have got lots of company today. C. J. Compton and wife is here. Mate and Frank Stilwell are here and Elmer and Marion Mathews are here. We went to meeting in the morning.

March, Monday 8. 1880.
We did not wash today. Wallace went to Logan and got me 3 yards of pink cloth for an apron. Henry went a-hunting. Pa went to Watkins. Em Stone and Jac Smith was here.

March, Tuesday 9. 1880.
I got breakfast. There is a nite party to Isaiah Strater [Strader] tonite. Tim VanWormer is here to work. Wallace and Ernest has gon to mill. Will Rudy and Parson Loose stayed all nite, last nite – here.

March, Wednesday 10. 1880.
We tended [attended] the ---- last nite. There wasn't many here. O. [Orville] Townsend wanted to fetch me home. I won't tell the reason rite here but Charley Saterly was there. It was the first time I saw him.

March, Thursday 11. 1880.
I got breakfast. Ada washed yesterday. There is two men here a-sawing shingles. Eva Weaver is here. Ed has gone to singing school. Will Rudy is here all the time to work.

March, Friday 12. 1880.
I got breakfast this morning. There has been 16 teams drawing logs here today. Jason Loose was here. Mate and Frank was over to Stilwell's and Frank came over here and stayed a little while.

March, Saturday 13. 1880.
Mate and Frank is here. Frank has gon to Logan and Mate is here. Will Rudy stayed all the nite. Ma red all the evening to us. Ed did not go to singing school last nite because he worked to late.

Ida Burnett

March, Sunday 14. 1880.
We did not go to meeting in the morning nor at nite. There was 2 fellows here to dinner. Carrie looked for George but he did not come. Pa went up to Frank's. Wallace and Ernest went with him.

March, Monday 15. 1880.
I and Ada washed. Carrie don the housework. Frank was here to dinner. I and Ada went down and got up steam and whistled for the men to come to dinner. Tim VanWarmer was here.

March, Tuesday 16. 1880.
Will Gittens is here this forenoon and got canfull of Jell. They start for Geneva tomorrow. I and Carrie went up to Smith's a-visiting. Carrie and --- gave us their pictures.

March, Wednesday 17. 1880.
Mate and Frank has been here all day. Pary [Perry] Brown was here and asked Ada to go to the party Saturday with him. She is a-going. I made some ginger snaps. ----- and ------- are here.

March, Thursday 18. 1880.
Wallace has been down to ------- Hall's a--------- after butter and he got the mail - a letter for me, Carrie, Ada, and Henry. All from George Baker. He wants us to come over Saturday.

March, Friday 19. 1880.
Frank Stilwell ran the saw. Pa and Henry went after some straw. I popped some corn. Ada and Wallace went to Logan.

March, Saturday 20. 1880.
Pa and Henry went to Watkins. Pary come after Ada but he did not do enough to get out and help her in the Shelton [brand of carriage]. Wallace went a-horseback. Pa and Henry got one a pair of shoes and 3 ruffles.

March, Sunday 21. 1880.
We went to meeting this morning. Jason Loose was here all day. Carrie went up home with the Mathews girls and stayed all nite. Pa schollded [scolded].

MARCH, FRIDAY 19. 1880.

Frank Stilwell run the saw. Pa and Henry went after some straw. I roped some corn fodder and Wallace went to house we got them with a load of wood.

SATURDAY 20.

Pa and Henry went to Mathews. Polly came after Ada but she could not no enough to get out and help her in the skeliton. Wallace went to horsemill. Pa and Henry got me a pair of shoes and 3 rufflest.

SUNDAY 21.

We went to meeting this morning Jason &c was here all day. Every went ap home with Mathews girls and stayed all nite. Pa scholded.

March, Monday 22. 1880.
I and Ada washed. Carrie got home tonite. Elmer and Marion brought her and spent the evening. Ada went home with Mate. Cara Jonson was here from Berdett [Burdett] to get the school.

March, Tuesday 23. 1880.
Carrie got breakfast. I packed shingles all day – packed twenty bunches and earned 50 sents. There was lots of men to the mill. Ada has not got back yet. Henry -----his colt today.

March, Wednesday 24. 1880.
I have packed shingles all day today – packed 6 thousand – earned 60 sents. Ada has not got home yet. Henry has gon over to Reynoldsville to take Mr. Malone over. Ezekell Compton called a little while.

March, Thursday 25. 1880.
Ada got home from Mate's today and went to up Couse's and got some buttermilk. Niles and Dave Devit was here and I made --- cakes and they ate 6 a piece.

March, Friday 26. 1880.
I got breakfast. Carrie and Ada nor Ma did not get up until 8 o'clock. Just as I got dinner ready Frank Chandler and Ida Howell come – ate dinner and stayed all nite. Carrie slept with them. Mate and Frank has been here all day.

March, Saturday 27. 1880.
Ida went home this morning. Mate and Frank are here again. Mate, Frank, I and Carrie went down to Jessie's and stayed all day. We had a little calf born today. Frank stayed all nite tonite.

March, Sunday 28. 1880.
Today is Easter Sunday – I ate 8 eggs for breakfast – then did not any of us go to meeting this morning nor at nite. Henry, Carrie and myself went to Tim's and stayed all day.

March, Monday 29. 1880.
I and Ada washed all day. Frank S. was here to dinner. Henry and Wallace are very sick. Henry went to Logan to get the paper and Carrie a letter and lost them.

March, Tuesday 30. 1880.
Wallace and Henry puked all over the house last nite. Pa saw Jason L. and he found the mail and give it to him.

March, Wednesday 31. 1880.
I got up sick and laid a-bed all day. Henry is better – he went over after the men to cut shingels but they did not come. Carrie rote to George today.

April, Thursday 1. 1880.
Carrie was 17 today. Miss Carrie VanDoren was here today and settled up. There was a man here all day waiting for Pa to come home from Odessa. M---- and Carrie Compton was here this afternoon. Mate is here all day.

April, Friday 2. 1880.
Mate and Frank stayed all nite last nite. Ada has gon to North Hector [now Valois, NY] with them to help them move. Will Rudy went and drove one team. Ma went up to Smith's and stayed all day. Will Gittens was here all day. Mate and Frank stayed all nite. Ed was 13 today.

April, Saturday 3. 1880.
There is a man here a-sawing shingles from Reynoldsville. We have got chickens for dinner. Fred and George Baker are here. Fred went to Mary ---'s and wanted me to go with him but did not. George stayed all nite.

April, Sunday 4. 1880.
It reigned so last nite that we didn't go to up to Dickenson's as intended. Henry went and took George up today. Avery Thomas is here all day. We had mush and milk tonite.

April, Monday 5. 1880.
I got breakfast. I and Ada washed. When we got throu Ada went to the mill and packed 2000 shingles. Will red all of the evening. Mrs. Rich died today. Frank Stilwell was here to dinner.

April, Tuesday 6. 1880.
I got breakfast – ironed all day long. Ma, Carrie, and Ada all went to the funeral. They said there wasn't many there. Ada has packed shingles all day today. Ed was up and got some milk.

April, Wednesday 7. 1880.
Pa found a little calf all buried up in shit behind the bull - it belonged to the heffer. I lost on a bet with Henry about getting on Wallace's boot.

April, Thursday 8. 1880.
Manroe Kingsley was here to dinner. He has got our chest [?] moste done. Carrie and I went up to Couse's a-visiting. We --- an interduction to Arthur Connolly. Pa and Ernest went to Watkins. We started to Smith's when we come back.

April, Friday 9. 1880.
We had fresh fish for breakfast. Ma and Ada went up to the minister's visiting. Carrie took them and I went after them. No I didn't but I wanted to. Wallace did.

April, Saturday 10. 1880.
Henry and Will Rudy went to Watkins. They did not get back very early. Jasson Loose was here. Jane Weaver was here two times. Florence and Mattie Bond was here. Mate and Frank came up and stayed all nite. Jane took Henry's papers home with here. There was lots of them.

April, Sunday 11. 1880.
Will stayed all nite. Frank went over to his foakses [folks] and stayed all nite. Arthur Connolly and another fellow are hired and stayed all nite. Mate stayed all nite too. I will go down and work for the Mekeels.

April, Monday 12. 1880.
We did not go to meeting yesterday atall [at all]. Frank come back today

and him and Mate went home. Jason was here again. We did not wash to day because it was so cold. George worked all day today.

April, Tuesday 13. 1880.
Sattie VanWarmer stayed all nite here last nite and to breakfast. Carrie Mekeel and her brother was here and wanted me to go and work for them and I am a-going. I go to Mr. Mekeel's next Monday.

April, Wednesday 14. 1880.
I have commenced doing the milking now. I and Carrie went to Logan and I got me 2.31 sents worth of things. I washed a little. Carrie ironed, Ada washed the sealen [ceiling].

April, Thursday 15. 1880.
I hain't done much today but sow on my dress. Carrie made one of my aprons and almoste the hull [whole] of the other one. Ada stayed all nite with Sattie VanWarmer last nite. She was down to Jones's.

April, Friday 16. 1880.
I finished my dress and aprons today. Ma done the moste of the housework today. Carrie ran the engine and Ada packed shingles. There was a man here to dinner from Baltimore. He was a phosphate agent.

April, Saturday 17. 1880
I don a little washing this morning. Ada don my ironing while I and Carrie went up to Smith's and helped them quilt. They sent Orville after us. Will milked for me tonite. Pa has gon to Logan. I am going away tomorrow. Jason is here.

April, Sunday 18. 1880.
Jason stayed all nite last night and so did Will Rudy. We all went to meeting this morning. Willie Menetton was here to dinner.

April, Monday 19. 1880.
Mate and Frank came after me. I am up to Mekeel's [in North Hector – now Valois, NY] now and I am afraid I will be home sick. I washed today. Mate was up here this morning. There has been lots of fokes [folks] here today. I let the sheep out of the barn.

APRIL, SUNDAY 18. 1880.

Jason stayed all nite last night and so did Will Rud[?] we all went to meeting this mornin Willie McNelton [?] were to dinner [?]

MONDAY 19.
I [?] to [?] [?]
[?] [?]
Will be here sick
I wanted to [?]
[?] was up here
this morning. [?]
has been lots of [?]
here to [?] [?]
sheep [?] [?] [?] soon

TUESDAY 20.
I churned [?] and
made a batch of ginger-
snaps. [?] [?] [?]
and at supper I [?]
[?] nite with her last
nite and [?] nite. I
started after the mail
and got a[?] [?]
was there and left the
[?] with it.

April, Tuesday 20. 1880.
I churned, ironed and made a batch of ginger snaps. Mate was here and ate supper. I stayed all nite with her last night. I started after the mail and got a-fourth way there and met Mate with it.

April, Wednesday 21. 1880.
I did not get here until breakfast was ready. There was a lady stayed all nite here last nite. Mrs. Mekeel was to [a] funeral and I got dinner and was down to Mate's all of the afternoon.

April, Thursday 22. 1880.
We cleaned the sullor [cellar] today and I am moste tired to death. I have got an awful soar finger. I hain't seen Mate today.

April, Friday 23. 1880.
We cleaned the ---- and I am more tired than I was last nite. There has been a woman here all day and another one once but she came in the morning and stayed all day so I hain't much help.

April, Saturday 24. 1880.
I done up the Saturday's work and Frank went down to the burg and found Mr. ---- there and he stayed to dinner. Then I and Mate and him went home and stoped to Poly's. Met Pa after him.

April, Sunday 25. 1880.
I stayed nite. Went to meeting. Henry and 4 of the girls. Jason Loose was there. Ernest's horse had a colt. We stayed to supper and then came home to Mekeel's.

April, Monday 26. 1880.
Mate was up the day before yesterday and I am a-going in a minute. I washed and set the close [clothes] to soak because it reigned. Mate come up so I did not come down.

April, Tuesday 27. 1880.
I hung up the close and ironed the moste of them. Mate was up again and she wants me to get a dollar of Mekeel and lend it to her but I don't want to very bad.

April, Wednesday 28. 1880.
We have done moste every thing to day. Made soap and baked bread and Katie was here all day. Mrs. Mekeel fell down and liked to busted her arse. I wanted to laff.

April, Thursday 29. 1880.
I was down to Mate's yesterday and she was up here today. I broak the chimney damper and the cow got in and bent the pale [pail].

April, Friday 30. 1880.
Mrs. Mekeel sent me down to Mate's with a pail of soap – she gave it to her. There was a man here to dinner and a little boy. The cow run and liked to broak her neck.

May, Saturday 1. 1880.
I done up the work and pieced or finished piecing a --------. I broak a tumbler. Waisted a sip of mustard. Mate came up and I went down and stayed all nite.

May, Sunday 2. 1880
I come home and done up the work. Changed my close and went down again. Will, Henry, Carrie and Ada and Wallace come and stayed all day. We went to the lake and took a ride on the watter.

May, Monday 3. 1880.
I washed. Katie stayed all nite and all day but she hated to go home real bad. I felt sorrow for her and I am again lend her my books this summer.

May, Tuesday 4. 1880.
We got up really early and have cleaned the parlor. Mate has been up three times. Mr. Mekeel went over to the lake and was moste tired to death when he got back. I'd like to go home.

May, Wednesday 5. 1880.
I stayed all nite with Mate last nite. They was a-eating when I got there. I broak the close stick. There was a man here to supper. Mate was up tonite. Frank's horse has got a colt.

May, Thursday 6. 1880.
How mad the old lady was when she found a tack in every side of the carpet. We cleaned the setting room today. Mr. Mekeel went to Watkins. I am real tired and I guess I will go down to Mate's.

May, Friday 7. 1880.
Mrs. Mekeel gave me a role [roll] of calicoes and a pair of cuffs. The hens all got to laying in one nest or Mekeel thought so at least, but I was to blame. There was a terrible time about it. Mate and Frank has gone home.

May, Saturday 8. 1880.
They want me to stay three years with them. He says that he will give me a cow and she says she will make a wedding when I get married up if I marry to suit them, but donte think I will stay. There was to [two] men here to supper.

May, Sunday 9. 1880.
I went down to the burgh yesterday. Mate and Frank has got back. I was down there and stayed all day. Pa is sick. Ed Ely has been here all of the evening and I donte know what to think of it.

May, Monday 10. 1880.
We did not wash today. Frank has gon up home to stay all the rest of the week. Mate is a-going to stay with me every night. I forgot to put any tea in the teapot and there was quite a time about it.

May, Tuesday 11. 1880.
I washed. The old lady has worked in the garden all day. Mate come up and got some plants. Mrs. Mekeel has gon to bed. Fannie rode up from the burgh with Irvin Moore.

May, Wednesday 12. 1880.
I ironed. Pa was down to mill and he stayed to Mate's. I would liked to go home with him. I fixed my stockings and it took me all of the afternoon. She gave me the pieces.

Ida Burnett

May, Thursday 13. 1880.
We have got a very sick horse. Fannie has been here today. I guess I will go home Sunday. I was down to Mate's this morning and took her some seads [seeds].

May, Friday 14. 1880.
I shot a crow but he got away. We cleaned part of the kitchen and went down to Mate's and all of the afternoon Mr. Mekeel went to Watkins on the stage. I heared a noise in the suller [cellar] and got scared.

May, Saturday 15. 1880.
Mate has stayed with me every nite this week. I wanted to go home but cannot. I have been here four weeks now. They try to please me but they cannot so let them try.

May, Sunday 16. 1880.
I stayed all nite with Mate and to breakfast. C--- and Mattie was there. Fannie is here. There was a tramp here and got his supper. I would have liked to gone home today but could not.

May, Monday 17. 1880.
I washed and was down to Mate's agan. Mrs. Mekeel says I can go home whenever I want to go. I guess I will go a-horse back next Saturday. Her daughter is coming then.

May, Tuesday 18. 1880.
I ironed and done some bakeing. She works in the garden the most of the time. They bragged on my pie. Mr. Mekeel lost his knife.

May, Wednesday 19. 1880.
I finished the ironing and went down and sprouted the potatoes that was down to Mate's and looked for the knife. Frank went up home yesterday. Mate is staying with me agan.

May, Thursday 20. 1880.
We cleaned the kitchen today – it has done something today that it has tried to do for many a day – that it reigned, it haled a little. Mate is up here and a-singing.

May, Friday 21. 1880.
We're a-fixing to come home tomorrow. I am a-going to brake the little colt or my neck. I hain't certain which. I took a horseback ride. Mate was here to supper. I went down to the burgh.

May, Saturday 22. 1880.
Carrie and Mrs. Terry came over. Henry, Ada, Mary and Martha came down after me. I went up home with them. We met George on the corner and he went back with us.

May, Sunday 23. 1880.
They went home. Ed got there just as they went away. He would have liked to see them very much. Our foakse [folks] had lots of company. Mr. Mekeel came after me and when we got here she had the head-acke.

May, Monday 24. 1880.
Mrs. Mekeel is very sick and I did not work today. Mate come up and stayed all night. There is a couple of ladies here. One is family.

May, Tuesday 25. 1880.
Fannie come up and helped me wash. She is a pretty good girl. I have folded the clos [clothes] and have an awful ironing for tomorrow.

May, Wednesday 26. 1880.
Mr. Mekeel took my shoes down last nite to get them fixed and got me too spools of thread to fix over my grean dress. She has gon up home with Whitley Smith. I hope she will have a nice time.

May, Thursday 27. 1880.
I went down to the burg last night and got me a buckel [buckle] for my hat, a couple of hare [hair] pins. It was two shillings and the pins was a penny a piece.

May, Friday 28. 1880.
Mr. Mekeel got my shoes but they did not pay for them. We picked the potato bugs and tied up grapes. It liked to make me sick.

May, Saturday 29. 1880.
We tied up grapes what time we got. Mate and Frank got back. Wallace went home.

May, Sunday 30. 1880.
I stayed all nite with Mate. Wallace was up three or four times. Mate is a-going to fix over dresses this week. I hope he won't lick brick for staying so long.

May, Monday 31. 1880.
I washed and got it all out at 8 o'clock. We tied up grapes the rest of the day. Mate is a-staying all night.

June, Tuesday 1. 1880.
Mate come up and helped me iron. I was down there all of the afternoon. We went down to the village. They [the Mekeels] had company today.

June, Wednesday 2. 1880.
There was a woman gave me a letter. Mate done her collars today. I went down and tried on my dress tonite.

June, Thursday 3. 1880.
Carrie come down this morning and stayed all day. I went down to Mate's with her. Carrie Smith is here tonite and I guess that the old lady is a-going home with her.

June, Friday 4. 1880.
Mr. Mekeel went home with Carrie to stay until Sunday. Mate has been up here pretty much all day. I am a-going to stay all nite with her.

June, Saturday 5. 1880.
I have had to work pretty hard today. Henry and Pa was here to dinner. Henry started for Geneva but Pa come after him and got him to go back with him.

This view is on the corner of Logan and Mathews Roads, looking east on Mathews Road. Ida's home was within view just past the pine tree on the right. Photograph by Allen C. Smith, 2008.

June, Sunday 6. 1880.
I stayed all nite and when I got up here Mekeel had breakfast all ready. I went back and stayed all day. They brought the laundry home with them.

June, Monday 7. 1880.
They brought a lot of dirtie close over here for me to wash. Mr. and Mrs. Andrews was here. I went down to Mate's in the evening. She has got my dress moste done.

June, Tuesday 8. 1880.
We had another caller. I and Mate went down to the burg. The cat liked to kill my [pet] bird. Mate finished my dress and it is splended.

June, Wednesday 9. 1880.
We had company agan today but I hope we won't agan this week. I am a-going home Saturday. If I go home Henry is there. Mate was up twice.

June, Thursday 10. 1880.
I and Mate tied grapes all day.

June, Friday 11. 1880.
We did not do much work today but tie grapes and I never will work in them agan.

June, Saturday 12. 1880.
We finished the grapes and Mr. Mekeel gave Mate $2.00 for what she done. I went down to Mate's.

June, Sunday 13. 1880.
Marrion and Carrie Smith came over today and Carrie is a-going to stay a week. I am certain they had lots of company today. I went down to Mate's and stayed a long time.

June, Monday 14. 1880.
I wanted to go home this week real bad but could not. I am going next

Saturday if I go a-foot for I want to see Henry. I hope he went home with Pa. Good nite dear diary.

June, Tuesday 15. 1880.
Katie was here and she hated to go home real bad agan. I feel real bad for the children anyhow. I went down to Mate's a little while. I am going home next Sunday nite.

June, Wednesday 16. 1880.
I ironed. Mrs. M. and her daughter went a-visiting and the foaks ----- at home. There was a woman brought my bird home tonite I was very glad.

June, Thursday 17. 1880
They had company and are agan tonite have more. Saturday and Sunday they want me to stay over but I don't think I will very much. I was down to Mate's.

June, Friday 18. 1880.
We are fixing for company. Mate took Birdie home with her. I have packed cherries all day.

June, Saturday 19. 1880.
Their company did not come as expected. I am waiting for the horse and Mate to go home. Carrie fixed my hare.

June, Sunday 20. 1880.
When we got home all of the Enfield fooks [folks] was there. Fred and Mary ------ came down this morning. We went to church. I had to give two fellows the mutin [mutton?] agan. Sore back side.

June, Monday 21. 1880.
I am tired all moste to death and got a sore bottom. I had to work like everything. I went down to Mate's. Miss my bird.

June, Tuesday 22. 1880.
I ironed all day. They had a lot of company. Mate has been down twice. My bottom hain't got [better] but it is a-coming slowly.

June, Wednesday 23. 1880.
She wanted I should tie grapes but that has played out. I hain't a-going to tie any more. I was down to Mate's a little while this evening.

June, Thursday 24. 1880.
Ma come down this morning and Henry and I have been down to Mate's all day. Ma gave Mate a pound of shugor [sugar]. I am homesick and would like to go home.

June, Friday 25. 1880.
I done worked pretty hard today. They had company. I was down to Mate's and she come up and helped me get some cherries.

June, Saturday 26. 1880.
I am glad that another week is gon for I have worked pretty hard. They donte any body know that I am homesick but I am a little. I was down to Mate's and she was up here.

June, Sunday 27. 1880.
I have done all of their work today. The hired man come to stay all nite. Abram [Mr. Mekeel] milked tonite. I done a little patterning and was down to Mate's.

June, Monday 28. 1880.
I washed and took a map and went a------ and got all of the fooks a-looking for me but I was down to Mate's a-talking about going out west. She is staying all nite with me.

June, Tuesday 29. 1880.
I have picked berries all day about one bushel. Sat down in a bees' nest and got stung pretty bad. They were yellow jackets with pretty large stingers.

June, Wednesday 30. 1880.
We finished picking the cherries. I was down to Mate's. We would like to go home the Forth [Fourth of July] but cannot. My limb is swelled awful tonight where the sting is.

July, Thursday 1. 1880.
I picked a few berries and Abe Mekeel tries to interest me about a fellow that is to work here. Mate was up all of the afternoon.

July, Friday 2. 1880.
I picked berries all day and was fearful tired. I went down to Mate's and took my patching along. Frank was sick all day.

July, Saturday 3. 1880.
All of our foaks come down and we went down to North Hector. They had two pretty good fites [fights] – it was good to see them. I had to give a fellow the milking. They say O. Baker won't live long.

July, Sunday 4. 1880.
I am to home. Come up with them last night. Henry brought me home. The church got a-fire. Will R got drunk. There was six stayed all night. Frank took Will's watch and he was mad.

July, Monday 5. 1880.
I washed. Mate was up. I had a good time home and am sorrow that we are a-going to loose a very kind and good brother in 3 months.

July, Tuesday 6. 1880.
Mate was up three times – I was down once. Dan Molton is here a-trying to blast that body out of the lake that got [drowned] on Saturday. I hope that he will get it.

July, Wednesday 7. 1880.
I washed the white close. ------ was here to dinner, but I did not eat with them. I learned yesterday that he was only twenty although he looks 40. I am a-mending my stockings.

July, Thursday 8. 1880.
I hain't worked very hard today but I broak a lamp. Mrs. Mekeel went to the burg and got me a corset. Mate was up all of the afternoon.

JULY, SUNDAY 11. 1880.

I churned this morning
Poe and the three
little boys was
down last night
went home with
them Mate felt
very bad but came
home with out
me

MONDAY 12.

I washed and hung
out to make a plum
pudding for
dinner I was afraid
it wont be good
I went down to the
store got 2 lamb chim-
and Mate & Jessie back
come

TUESDAY 13.

Mate stayed all of
the fore noon she
is a going home
in the stage in
the morning I
seen and heard
Hervey to make
I did not say
any or drink.

July, Friday 9. 1880.
They had company. I had to pick currants for them all afternoon. Mate helped me. I am awful tired. It is pleasant but real hot.

July, Saturday 10. 1880.
I have been here 12 weeks now and wish my time was up but it is not. 8 more weeks to stay. I hain't a-doing milk this afternoon.

July, Sunday 11. 1880.
I churned this morning. Pa and the three little boyes was down and Frank went home with them. Mate felt real bad but come up and stayed with me.

July, Monday 12. 1880.
I washed and have got to make a pudding for dinner. I am afraid it won't be good. I went down to the burg and got a lamp and Mate a dressing comb.

July, Tuesday 13. 1880.
Mate stayed all of the foornoon [forenoon]. She come home in the stage in the morning. I went down to Mate's. ------- went by awful drunk.

July, Wednesday 14. 1880.
Mate went up home on the stage and I hope she will have a nice time. Poly and Frank went last evening. He cut his finger and I have got to Mate's.

July, Thursday 15. 1880.
It has been kind of lonesome without Mate. There was an awful thunderstorm last night. I pitted cherries all day. Dr. Johnson has got them here.

July, Friday 16. 1880.
I hain't worked very hard. I will be glad when I get out on the roaling prairie if I ever get there and I hope I may. I will be glad when Mate gets home.

A four-corner panorama of Ida's crossroads, summer 2008. Photograph by Allen C. Smith.

July, Saturday 17. 1880.
Mr. Mekeel went away – Mrs. Mekeel went up to Hall's to make a call and I am here alone. A gobbler [turkey] got after me and I had to run like sixty.

July, Sunday 18. 1880.
Mate come home and brought me a pair of shoes, a shawl, and a pair of gloves. I took the horse and went up home. Carrie and I went to meeting and then I brought it [the horse] back again.

July, Monday 19. 1880.
I washed, picked blackberries. I was up to Mate's a little while and Frank offered me a week to stay at Mate's. I donte think I will, but she won't come up here.

July, Tuesday 20. 1880.
I ironed and picked a few berries and went down to the burg and ---- Stoped at Mate's sence [since] she is a-staying alone.

July, Wednesday 21. 1880.
It rained. Mate was up and got some currants. Mr. Mekeel went to Watkins. Mate is a-going to stay alone tonite.

July, Thursday 22. 1880.
Mate was up all day. Mrs. Mekeel went to the burg and solde some currants and got me a pair of slippers. The boss is terrible. I have to pick the currants.

July, Friday 23. 1880.
I hain't seen Mate today. There was company to dinner and 8 to supper. It would have been pleasant if it had not rained.

July, Saturday 24. 1880.
Mate was up 2 times. I went to the burg. The old yellow cow stepped on my hand and hurt it pretty bad. I guess I will go to church tomorrow.

July, Sunday 25. 1880.
We did not go to meeting – they both went away. I was down to Mate's. ---- got mad at Frank last Friday. I am a-going to sleep. I stay 4 weeks more.

July, Monday 26. 1880.
I washed. I and Mrs. Mekeel has been here all alone all day. We had quite a time getting the chickens. Mate was up and helped.

July, Tuesday 27. 1880.
We have commenced drying apples and I have to set in the kitchen all alone every afternoon and feel bad. I hain't got my foaks. Mate was up and I was down.

July, Wednesday 28. 1880.
Mate was up twice. I was a-helping get in the chickens and the old woman got mad. Irvin Moore went fast.

July, Thursday 29. 1880.
They hain't happened today but 2 old hens got out and Mate was up all day and Mrs. M [Mekeel] don't want me to go to school this winter.

July, Friday 30. 1880.
Mr. Mekeel commenced plowing today. Mate was up a minute. The Millimans had a picnic today. Henry to go west after all – I shall feel awful when he starts.

July, Saturday 31. 1880.
Mate was up and I was down. I went to ------ and wore Mrs. Mekeel's blue shoes. I took them off before. Charley and Frank said that Charley Baker was a-dying.

August, Sunday 1. 1880.
I have been down to Mate's all day and herd her reed [read]. I did not come in time to milk.

August, Monday 2. 1880.
I washed and Katie Tailor [Taylor?] come. Her father turned her out of dores [outdoors]. She is agan to stay all nite and so had an awful start.

August, Tuesday 3. 1880.
Katie has gon to Watkins to live. Mate was up. Never knew Mrs. Mekeel to speeke a pleasant word after breakfast in my life. Katie thought my shale [shawl] was splended.

August, Wednesday 4. 1880.
I picked four bushels of apples. It is rainy now. I have broak a fine plate, a soap plate, a big plate, and a pitcher this week.

August, Thursday 5. 1880.
It seams all moste like fall it is so cold. Mr. Mekeel has got an awful lame back and is moste sick. Mate is a-going home in the morning and I wish I was a-going to [too].

August, Friday 6. 1880.
Mate went before I was up. Mr. and Mrs. Mandeville is here. We are rite to the drying apples. I am a-going get me a pair of walking shoes.

August, Saturday 7. 1880.
We are a-cleaning up. Pa gone down to mill and brought Mate a---. I went home with him and he stopped on the road and bought a jack-ass.

August, Sunday 8. 1880.
We intended to go over to Baker's today but did not. I went to meeting and down to Jones's. Mr. Mekeel come after me very late.

August, Monday 9. 1880.
I washed. Mate was up and I am a-going down. Carrie and I are a-reading - each of us a story. The name of hers is "Eva May" and mine is "Jack and Minnie at the ----."

August, Tuesday 10. 1880.
Mr. Mekeel is out sick a-bed. We pealed apples all day and have about 5 bushels dried.

August, Wednesday 11. 1880.
Mate was up all day but did not eat. Mr. Mekutchen is a-going to Rochester. Only 5 weeks before Henry goes.

August, Thursday 12. 1880.
Mate was up all of the forenoon and got some corn ---- and -----. We are a-canning plums and the grapes are ripe – full of business on all sides.

August, Friday 13. 1880.
I never was so tired in my life. Frank is home sick with the side ake [ache]. I went down to the burg and got Mate a book, some shugar, and writing paper.

August, Saturday 14. 1880.
I was sick all nite last nite and when Mrs. Mekeel found it out she doctored me up and put red flannel all over me [red flannel was believed to prevent sickness and aid healing]. I squalled all of the evening.

August, Sunday 15. 1880.
I did not get up until noon and went down to Mate's. Ada and Wallace was there all day and they wanted I should go up home with them and stay a week but I could not.

August, Monday 16. 1880.
I donte feel very well today but I washed and Carrie and her man and Lulu was here. All day she kissed me when she went away.

August, Tuesday 17. 1880.
I think I am better although I have to [take] lots of metison [medicine]. Mate was up and stayed to supper. She worked all the time. I ironed and peeled apples.

August, Wednesday 18. 1880.
Mate was up and I was down. I took here some milk but Mrs. Mekeel hated to send it to her. Fannie is here. I am better of my colde.

August, Thursday 19. 1880.
It raigned all day but we had company just the same. They were Quakers – they come when I got supper all ready so I had to go to the burg.

August, Friday 20. 1880.
It has rained all day. Mate borrowed 5 sents of me and I went down to the burg and got her a book and the mail. Fannie is here and will stay all night.

August, Saturday 21. 1880.
Wallace and Ernest came down to mill and tolde me that Uncle David and Aunt Mary was there. So I went to the Mathews and rode up with Whitley Smith.

AUGUST, MONDAY 16. 1880.

I don't feel very
well to day but
I up and [...]
another [...]
[...] here
all day she kissed
me [...] she
[...]

TUESDAY 17.

I think I am [...]
although I have to take
lots of medison
Mate was [...]
[...] to Stampers
She worked all
of [...]
[...]

WEDNESDAY 18.

Mate was up and I
was down, [...]
[...] milk but
[...]
[...] sent it
[...] Annie is
here I am better
[...]

August, Sunday 22. 1880.
The house has ben full of company all day. Henry, Carrie, Ada and Frank brought me home. Stephen S., Henry and his girl were here.

August, Monday 23. 1880.
I washed and Mate was up and wanted I should go down to the burg for her. She said that he hadn't had a thing to eat since morning. I am awful tired.

August, Tuesday 24. 1880.
Carrie Mason and another family was here all day. I hulled elderberries until 9 o'clock. Then Mrs. Mekeel came and made me stop.

August, Wednesday 25. 1880.
My trouble is grate. Frank is so mean to Mate, but the worst of all is Henry's going away. I am almoste crazy and shall be when he is gone. I ironed all day. Mate was up.

August, Thursday 26. 1880.
Carrie come over and left Lulu [Andrews]. It has rained all day. Mate was up and I went down and stayed all nite with Mate.

August, Friday 27. 1880.
Mate was up a little while. My note is $20. Lulu is here yet and she is the ugliest thing I ever saw. She let a fart tonite.

August, Saturday 28. 1880.
Mr. Mekeel went to a pool raseing [political pole raising]. I went down to the burg. I am going down to stay with Mate. Lulu is here yet and Mate too.

August, Sunday 29. 1880.
Carrie was over. I was down to Mate's all day and tonite. Will Ballard come there and I rode out with him. We went to his foakes and did not get in till 11 o'clock.

August, Monday 30. 1880.
It has been nice today with everybody. It raigned. I worked but did not end up the closer. Mate came up and I went home with her and stayed all night.

August, Tuesday 31. 1880.
It was awful hard work to get up this morning. Mrs. Mekeel has been away all day. Mate was up. Abe has been away. I wish that Henry wasent going away.

September, Wednesday 1. 1880.
The Republicans raised a pole. There was one man here to dinner and three to supper. Mate was up all of the afternoon. Henry starts 3 weeks from Monday for the West.

September, Thursday 2. 1880.
We peeled apples all day. Mate was up. The threshers will be here Saturday and I am glad of it. I hain't rote much in my place lately.

September, Friday 3. 1880.
Carrie, Ada, and Wallace came down. Ada is again to stay with Mate. Mate borrowed 75 cents of me. Ada was up and got some apples and some grapes.

September, Saturday 4. 1880.
I was down to Mate's and to the burg. Ada seemed to like it down here. Charlie Andrews is here once again and to stay all night. Mate Gittens just come from Geneva.

September, Sunday 5. 1880.
I didn't get up very early and the boss was mad. The thrashers come tomorrow. Mrs. Mekeel went over to Carrie's. Ada come up and helped me churn and is a-going to stay till night.

September, Monday 6. 1880.
I washed and got dinner for the thrashers. Mrs. Mekeel got back after dinner. Bob Yates's little boy is dead [Cyrus Yates age 4].

September, Tuesday 7. 1880.
It took us all of foornoon [forenoon] to get dinner – there were 14 men to dinner and 10 to breakfast. We are canning peaches. Pa was here a little while.

September, Wednesday 8. 1880.
The thrashers finished and went away. I hated to see Henry go but he did. I kissed my hand to them and said goodbye. I went to the village. We worked awful hard.

September, Thursday 9. 1880.
Abe hired a man to stay and sleep in the house. Ada was up and wanted I and Mrs. Mekeel to come down and set with them but she would not. Mate felt bad I know.

September, Friday 10. 1880.
We pealed apples all day and I went down to Mate's and stayed all night. The hired man -----in the evening.

September, Saturday 11. 1880.
Carrie and Marrion Smith are here to stay all night. I suppose that Ma and Carrie are looking for Henry tonight but they donte think of me down here. Ada was up twice.

September, Sunday 12. 1880.
I didn't get up until they ate breakfast. I took Lulu and went down to Mate's and stayed all day. When I was a-milking Will Ballard come and I couldn't make him know what "no" meant.

September, Monday 13. 1880
I just returned from the burg. Lulu Andrews, her father, and Mrs. Manning called here. They have been over to the lake a-visiting.

September, Tuesday 14. 1880.
Mate was up and has a fever. Abe went up and got Frank. I and Ada went after the Doctor. Frank went up and got Ma but she donte think Mate is very sick. The Dr. has been here twice and Frank has gon after him agan.

September, Wednesday 15. 1880.
I and Mrs. Mekeel peeled apples and she had company. I and Ada went down to the village. Ma patched my apron and stocking. Ada stayed all last night and tonight.

September, Thursday 16. 1880.
Ma is here to Mate's yet. She got homesick and patched my apron and stockings and now she is patching my dress. I and Mrs. Mekeel was down there.

September, Friday 17. 1880.
We pealed apples all day and night down to Mate's. Ada was up three times. That pretty boy was here to work. I wante to go home tomorrow but cant.

September, Saturday 18. 1880.
I was down to Mate's. Rote a little on my story [this diary]. Frank has gone after his mother. Ada stayed all nite with me. I sent for Carrie, Henry and Will to come down tomorrow.

September, Sunday 19. 1880.
Mrs. Mekeel had the head ake. Carrie and Frankie come down in afternoon. Carrie was here to supper. Mr. Border was here. Frank's mother and Fannie was to Frank's all day.

September, Monday 20. 1880.
I churned and washed. Mrs. Mekeel went down and washed the baby [Mate's baby?]. F. Stillwell is the meanest person on earth. We peeled peaches all the afternoon. Carrie red what I have rote yesterday.

September, Tuesday 21. 1880.
Ada is here to stay all nite. I was down to Mate's. Mrs. Mekeel picked up apples all the time I was gon.

September, Wednesday 22. 1880.
Pa and Frankie was to Mate's, but he didn't stop and see me. I will be left alone in the morning. Abe's foaks are going away. I am sorrow.

September, Tuesday 21. 1880.

Bela is here to stay all nite. I was down to mothers on bey. Mrs McKeeb picked up apples all the time I was gon. [illegible] is to work [illegible]

Wednesday 22.

Pa and Frankie was to Mothers but they dident stop and see me. Frank dr I is gone I will be left alone in the morning. Abes folks are going away over [illegible]

Thursday 23.

Mr and Mrs McKeel has gon and I am dore at a loss. Abe has come to stay all night with me. He begee me him cow apples. I give them some milk.

September, Thursday 23. 1880.
Mr. and Mrs. Mekeel has gone and I am here alone. Ada has come to stay all night with me. She helped me with the apples. I gave them some milk.

September, Friday 24. 1880.
There was a man came last nite after we got to bed and stayed all nite. Carrie Mekutchen [McCuahern] and Ada are staying all nite with me. We broke one lamp.

September, Saturday 25. 1880.
Mrs. Mekeel is over to Carrie's. Abe is awful pleasant this time his wife is gon. Charley Andrews and Lulu was here to tea and stayed until 10 o'clock.

September, Sunday 26. 1880.
Abe got up and got the horses, and milked the cows. Called me and went after Jennie. Done the work up and went down to Mate's and stayed all day. They have got home.

September, Monday 27. 1880.
It raigned a little this morning so we did not hang up the close. We gathered b--- all day. There is something else that I want to say but dare not. Oh dear, oh dear.

September, Tuesday 28. 1880.
It has raigned all day. I got the close up two times and they hain't dry yet. I donte no but they will be stole but I hope not. The men are cleaning up grain.

September, Wednesday 29. 1880.
It rained all day. Pa and Ernest went up to North Hector and brought me a letter. I am a-going home on Saturday. I guess I will stay all nite to Mate's. We played ucher in the evening.

September, Thursday 30. 1880.
We pealed apples and sorted out and covered them up every 5 minutes. I am staying all nite with Ada agan. Abe is awful good natured today.

Ida Burnett

October, Friday 1. 1880.
Wallace come up after Ada. She was moste tickled to death. They went rite to the party from here. Fannie was here today. I want to go home tomorrow. Mate was up today.

October, Saturday 2. 1880.
We went rite into the cleaning and Frank come up here and got me and we went home. Fred, George Baker, John and Charlie Stillwell were there in the evening. Fred stayed all night – the rest went home.

October, Sunday 3. 1880.
George, Martha, Mate come over this morning. Fred wanted I should ride down as far as Peach Orchard but I would not. He was coming to see Mary ----. Fan is here to stay all nite.

October, Monday 4. 1880
We did not wash but we went to the chestnut picking. Fan is here and is going to stay all nite. Abe has gon to a Republican meeting. Mrs. Mekeel red to me all of the evening.

October, Tuesday 5. 1880.
Mr. and Mrs. Mekeel went to meeting and Mrs. Carnal [Carman?] come home with them and stayed to supper. They all went to church agan in the evening. I stayed all nite with Mate. Frank is sick a-bed.

October, Wednesday 6. 1880.
Mr. Mekeel went to a Republican meeting and Mrs. Mekeel to church. I stayed at home and pealed apples. It reigned. I got awful wet going after the cows. I got a sore finger.

October, Thursday 7. 1880.
Mate and Arther was up and made us a visit. They stayed to supper. We finished the apples but we worked at them all of the evening. Abe and Mekutchen went to the pole raising.

October, Friday 8. 1880.
We went up to the other place and got about three forks of chestnuts. We got back half past twelve, got our dinner, and ate some cake. Mate was here.

October, Saturday 9. 1880.
Mrs. Mekeel went up and picked some chestnuts. We worked awful hard. Abe has gon to the village. Fan was here. I wish ---- would come down.

October, Sunday 10. 1880.
Abe and Shed went chestnutting. I looked for Henry a little but have not seen him. Mate and Frank has gon away. I have been a-writeing all day and am almoste tired to death.

October, Monday 11. 1880.
Mate and Frank has not got back yet. I don an awful big washing and sowed in the afternoon. Mrs. Mekeel wants I should stay all winter with them but I shan't.

October, Tuesday 12. 1880.
I got up all night sick. It reigned. Jennie did not go away as intended. We did not work very hard. Mate has not got back yet. I am afraid something has happened.

October, Wednesday 13. 1880.
Mrs. Mekeel went a-visiting and the boss was over to our house. They are a-going to have the pole raising Saturday. We have got an invitation. Mate is there.

October, Thursday 14. 1880.
We worked until 9 o'clock to get ready for me to go home. I am complaining now with soor feet - they are awful but I hope they will get better.

October, Friday 15. 1880.
I made some ginger cake and washed up the breakfast dishes then Ada come after me. She said she drove the buggie, but she dident. We went to a Democrat meeting.

October, Saturday 16. 1880.
Come home last nite and worked till 2 o'clock. Dressed 6 chickens and roosted [roasted] a pig. The pole went up splended. Mrs. Smith and Paul [?] was there. It reigned a little. There was 60 men and Mathews for one.

October, Sunday 17. 1880.
Mate and Frank come home last nite. It reigned. We went a-chestnutting. Henry brought me down in his carriage. Carrie Smith and Masson [Mason] are here. Charlie Andrews is going to teach Logan school.

October, Monday 18. 1880.
Carrie left Lulu – she will be coming to stay two weeks. I made her a presant [present] of a dol [doll]. Mate's baby is sick. We was all down there. We did not wash.

October, Tuesday 19. 1880.
Mrs. Mekeel has been sick all day. We sewed on Lulu's dools close [doll's clothes]. I wanted to go down to Mate's but I don't. Mrs. Mekeel made me a present of a lot of ruffles.

October, Wednesday 20. 1880.
We cleaned the parlor - while we was at it two men come and then Frank Chandler. She was to Mate's in the evening. I stayed all nite there. Mate is going to make my dress.

October, Thursday 21. 1880.
We cleaned the sitting room and the kitchen. Lulu brook [broke] her doll. Mate was up a minute. I am awful tired tonite. I will be glad when my time is over here.

October, Friday 22. 1880.
We hain't done much. I and Lulu went down to Mate's. Frank hain't been to work. When we come in from milking I found Fannie here. She dried the dishes.

October, Saturday 23. 1880.
Mrs. Mekeel hain't very well. Fan is here yet – she hurts Lulu 40 times a day. She fitted Mrs. Mekeel's dress. Blaked [blacked] the stove this afternoon. I wish I could see Henry.

October, Sunday 24. 1880.
I got up and done up the breakfast work and went down to Mate's. I loaned her a ring [?]. Fan is here yet. Abe takes a good deal of stock in her.

October, Monday 25. 1880.
We done a-two weeks of washing. I am a going to the burg and stay all nite with Mate. Abe went to Watkins. He said Pa and Brick [?] was there.

October, Tuesday 26. 1880.
We got all ready to paint. Pa went past fast – he did not stop. I went down to Mate's and stayed all nite, Abe took her some wood. Lulu is good.

October, Wednesday 27. 1880.
I ironed, painted the floor partly. Abe tries to get me to hurrah for Garfield. I wish that I was with Will and Henry tonite.

October, Thursday 28. 1880.
A man come and painted the kitchen floor. Fan was here. I went down and helped Mate put up a bed sted then she came up and stayed all of the afternoon. Marrion was here to dinner.

October, Friday 29. 1880.
The day has passed but slow. Mate has been up twice. She rote to Pa to come after me. She is going up next week. I went to the burg. Charlie Hager was a-washing windows. He is a splended fellow.

October, Saturday 30. 1880.
I hain't seen Mate today. We had company all night until after dinner. Mr. Mekeel took her over. I hope that Pa and Ma will come down tomorrow. Lulu sleeps with me.

October, Sunday 31. 1880.
I expected to go home but things happened so I hain't. Carrie and Marrion are her to stay all nite. They are gone to take Lulu home with them. I'm glad.

XXNovember, XXMonday 1. 1880XXXXXXXXXXXXXXXX
[Ida's X's] We didn't wash but stratened [straightened] around in the kitchen. It seams grate like living agon [again]. Mate and her baby come up this afternoon. I am a-going home with them.

November, Tuesday 2. 1880.
Today is lecton [Presidential Election] and the men has all gone down to it. Mate was agon home. I and Mrs. Mekeel are here alone. I am going to sleep with her.

November, Wednesday 3. 1880.
I went to the village – stopped to Mate's when I come back. The boyes [boys] has got back and I am glad of it. Our school commences next month. I am a-going down to Mate's.

November, Thursday 4. 1880.
I worked all of the foornoon as usual. In the afternoon Mrs. Mekeel went down to Mate's while I went to the burg. I got Mate's pattern book. Went and stayed with her all nite.

November, Friday 5. 1880.
I was a-bakeing a cake this morning when a pretty nice fellow come up to the door. Mrs. Mekeel grabbed him around the neck and liked to squese [squeeze] him to death – it was Matt.

November, Saturday 6. 1880.
I worked a half of a day. Then Mr. and Mrs. Mekeel brought me home. They stayed a while. I was come up a little while. Our fooks are cleaning house to a terrable rate.

November, Sunday 7. 1880.
Henry and Mary Dickerson come here last nite. Mary stayed with Ada. Henry come after her. Will and Snider come back. Our pole blowed down last night.

November, Monday 8. 1880.
I went down to ---- after Frank but he could not come over. Fooks are thrashing. Mate come up with her baby. I and she went to Frank. She is making my dress.

November, Tuesday 9. 1880.
Mate worked on my dress then we went to Hector. I payed Mrs. Boil [Boyle]. I and Carrie sent for correspondence on a book.

NOVEMBER, FRIDAY 5. 1880.

I was a baking a [cake] this morning when a pretty nice fellow come up to the door. Mrs ___ grabbed him ar[ound] the neck and [kissed?] him [...]

SATURDAY 6.

I worked a half of a day, then Mr and Mrs Mekeel brought me home. They stayed a little while. Some come [by] a little while [...] our [...] our [sleeping] house [...]

SUNDAY 7.

Henry and Mrs [...] come [...] [...] little [...] [...] to the [...] come [...] first will and [...] come back our [...] down [...]

November, Wednesday 10. 1880.
We did not go to Watkins. Pa went to Hector. Mrs. Seybold is here a-visiting. Henry and Will are gone to Logan.

November, Thursday 11. 1880.
Myself, Carrie and Henry went to Watkins. I got lots of [cavities] but did not get my teeth filled up. Wanted I should come on Saturday.

November, Friday 12. 1880.
I am a-going to [dentist] tomorrow. Frank Stillwell is here. I and Ada are fixing up our things to sleep upstares tonite.

November, Saturday 13. 1880.
I and Ada went to Watkins. I got my teeth filled. The man beete [beat] me out of $1.50. Mate and Frank are here to stay all nite.

November, Sunday 14. 1880.
I, Carrie and Ada went to meeting. Mate and Frank is here all day but are gon over to --------. Albert [?] is here. School commences a week from tomorrow.

November, Monday 15. 1880.
I and Carrie washed. Ada done the housework in the foornoon. Ma is fixing to go to Geneva. Were a peddler here and I bought a table spread $1.50.

November, Tuesday 16. 1880.
I and Ada done the housework. Ma's fixing to go to Geneva in the morning. I and Ada was down to Jones's for the redding of the newspaper.

November, Wednesday 17. 1880.
Our fooks fooled around until noon and then got started. I went down to Jones's and got cider. The boyes went a-hunting.

November, Thursday 18. 1880.
Irving Dunham and his boy was here yesterday. They are fixing to saw tomorrow. I went after Frank Chandler but he could not come.

November, Friday 19. 1880.
I and Carrie done up the farm work and then took the minister two chickens. Mate Gittens come along with us. Mate and Frank come and stayed all nite.

November, Saturday 20. 1880.
Mate and Frank went away before dinner. Our book that we sent for has come. Jane come up this afternoon. She would not take any part in the eggs.

November, Sunday 21. 1880.
They dident go to meeting. Will went home. Our foaks hain't got home yet. I did not finish my dress last evening.

November, Monday 22. 1880.
Carrie washed. I did the housework. S---'s little boy was sick and he went home but he come back. It is nite and our foaks have not returned. The boyes started to school.

November, Tuesday 23. 1880.
Carrie is making my dresses. We heard the news that the Colters [?] was sick and our foaks cant come home until they get well.

November, Wednesday 24. 1880.
The boyes got to school. Our foaks [arrived] home tonite. They got lots of news. They got Carrie a dress. We were eating supper when they came.

November, Thursday 25. 1880.
Today is Thanksgiving. I worked awful hard. Will Rudy is sick and so is Carrie and Hugh. Hugh is the best fellow. We got a new hired man.

November, Friday 26. 1880.
I and Carrie and Ada did up 2 -------. Mate and Frank are moving over to Reynoldsville. Mrs. Smith called here today.

November, Saturday 27. 1880.
Frank and Mate moved. My dress is not finnished yet and Mate left it here. I am a-going to finnish it myself. Charley Dates was here to dinner. Hugh has gone home.

November, Sunday 28. 1880.
Henry and Carrie went to meeting this morning. We looked for Will Edwards and his wife but they did not come.

November, Monday 29. 1880.
Carrie and I washed. I made me a pair of drawers after I got through washing. We fixed the dried apples to take to Watkins tomorrow. Pa is going to Geneva tomorrow.

November, Tuesday 30. 1880.
Mate and Frank finished moving. Ma, Carrie, and Ada went to Watkins. They got me fringe and a ribbon for my dress. Pa went to Geneva. Mate stopped here.

December, Wednesday 1. 1880.
Frankie is five years old. I and Carrie two of the four com----. The minister was here a little while then went down to Jones's. We only had 2 meals today.

December, Thursday 2. 1880.
I and Carrie made Ada two dresses. I finished mine but Carrie did not hers. Pa has not got back yet. I am afraid that he is sick. Ma and Ada done the housework.

December, Friday 3. 1880.
We are a-soing [sewing] on my dress. Pa and [?] did come when dinner was ready. I tell you dear diary. Henry went to Watkins.

December, Saturday 4. 1880.
I and Ada are doing the house work. Mate and Frank are gon [sic] to Watkins. Earl is here. We went up and see Carrie's baby. It is splended. Wallace went home with Mate.

December, Sunday 5. 1880.
I rained a little but went to meeting. Henry Boyd come home with us. Frank helped Ma do up all of the work.

December, Monday 6. 1880.
I commenced going to school. I think that Fred is the crossest teacher that I ever saw. I couldn't half study. Ernest is an awful youngen [young one].

December, Tuesday 7. 1880.
I went to school agan. The teacher is as cross as ever. Will McNetten got picked [up] out of his boots. Hugh and John [?] was here today.

December, Wednesday 8. 1880.
Fred was a little pleasanter. Charlie Mattison got whipped. I am lame tonite. I think that I will learn something this winter.

December, Thursday 9. 1880.
Fred was very pleasant. I went over to McNetten's –Willie is sick. When we got home Ma had gon over to Mate's – she is very sick. Dick brought the sulky home.

December, Friday 10. 1880.
I went to school. Fred was awful good today. When we got home Frank was here and I went home with him. There was a man there – it was Pid.

December, Saturday 11. 1880.
Frank come up this morning and said that Willis Rudy was dead. Henry set up with him. ---- Percy Jason was here to dinner. I doesn't go to bed.

December, Sunday 12. 1880.
Frank and Mate brought me home. Carrie is up to Rudy's. We all went up and seen Will – he looked natrel [natural]. They all feal real bad. I paid Mate $1.00.

December, Monday 13. 1880.
We all went to the furnal [funeral]. Mate was there and she went to the grave. Henry was one of the barers [pallbearers]. They stayed and got him [buried]. It was four o'clock when we got home.

December, Tuesday 14. 1880.
I and Ada washed. Will came back. I made me an apron. Charley Dates was here. Wallace went to North Hector and went to Abe Mekeel's and J---'s church.

December, Wednesday 15. 1880.
Carrie took us to school. Fred and Em is very sober. We walked home. Will is to work. He is taking music lessons. He feels real bad about Willis.

December, Thursday 16. 1880.
We drove the colts today. Henry drove so slow that we liked to froze to death. Em rode home with us. Fred wouldent [wouldn't ride home]. Will took another lesson to ------.

December, Friday 17. 1880.
We walked to school. I was taken sick tonite. Wallace went to Logan. Fred felt a little better.

December, Saturday 18. 1880.
I, Carrie, and Ada went to Watkins. Carrie made me a Christmas presant of a pair of earrings and box and a ring. Frank and Carrie is home. Hugh was here.

December, Sunday 19. 1880.
I was a-going home with Will but not last nite. I gave one of my pictures. Irving and B---- Moore come home with us.

December, Monday 20. 1880.
We went to school. Pid and Frank Stillwell was here. Fred and Em has got to feeling pretty well.

December, Tuesday 21. 1880.
We went to school. I hain't give Will his present yet. Pa and Jack Weaver went up on the mill and had one awful time.

December, Friday 17. 1880.

we walked to sch[ool]
I was taken sick
large mile. Lost
a [?] of my
sock. Mattie [went]
to Logan. I get
a little better

Saturday 18.

I carried [?] to sch[ool]
on the train. Cora
made me a christmas
present of [?]
ear rings and a
bracelet & [?]
Frank and Cora to
[?] sleigh [?]

Sunday 19.

[?] a [?] time
with will [?]
last nite. I gave one
of my [?] to [?]
[?] Daniel [?]
went to meeting
I win and [?]
moved and [?]
[?]

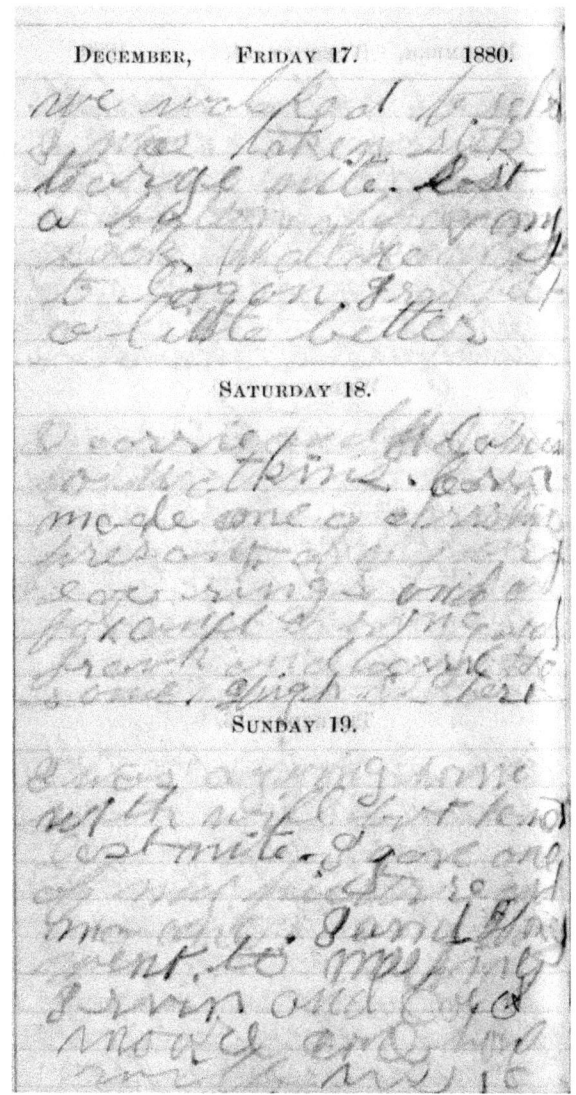

December, Wednesday 22. 1880.
We went to school agan. We have splended times. Em is jollie. The boyes are chopping the wood and us girls are piling it up. Henry went to Logan.

December, Thursday 23. 1880.
Wallace went after Poly and Frank. He gave me 8 cents for milking his cows. We went to school. Took a ----- with a parson.

December. Friday 24. 1880.
Henry took Poly home last night. Frank stayed. Henry took Frank to North Hector. He had to come home at recess. Charlie D, Will R, Henry E, and Frank S went to Reynoldsville.

December, Saturday 25. 1880.
Today is Chrismas. The boyes got there [their] stockings full. I and Wallace went to mill. I went to Mekeel's but there wasn't anyone home except Mrs. Mekeel – the rest had gone over to Grannie's [?] Henry and Will are went to Trumansburg. I made Will a present.

December, Sunday 26. 1880.
We all went to meeting. Henry and Carrie went up to Zeek's. Will hain't back yet it is awful lonesome. Henry got some oysters last night.

December, Monday 27. 1880.
We went to school but was late. A-coming home from school Fred put his arm around Ada's neck. There was a terrible time about it. Will gave me a knife.

December, Tuesday 28. 1880.
We all went to school but we came home at recess to go to the nite party. Abe Mekeel was here a little while. Carrie S. is sick and Mrs. Mekeel is over there. We got back at 12 o'clock.

December, Wednesday 29. 1880.
We went to school. We went up to Bell's at noon but Ida was not there. We had to stay in at recess. Em Rudy come home and stayed all night. We had lots of fun.

December, Thursday 30. 1880.
We went to school all day – it was awful cold. We like to frosed to death. We we got home we fixed up and went to Ida's to a party – we had a splended time.

December, Friday 31. 1880.
It is a little warmer this morning. Ida Bell and her lady friend visited the school. I, Ada and Em Rudy went up to Bell's and stayed until evening. John brought us home at 12.

Bibliography

Fenton, William E. "Laurel Hill Cemetery, Catharine, Schuyler County." 2002. Genweb. August 4, 2008 <http://www.rootsweb.ancestry.com/~nyschuyl/laurel.htm>.

Fenton, William E. "Glenwood Cemetery, Schuyler County, New York." 2001. Genweb. October 25, 2008 <http://www.rootsweb.ancestry.com/~nyschuyl/Glenwood.html>.

Howard, Helena. "Hector Presbyterian Cemetery, Hector, Schuyler County, New York." 2000. Genweb. September 11, 2008 <http://www.rootsweb.ancestry.com/~nyschuyl/hecpresb.htm>.

New York State censuses 1860-1920, Steele Memorial Library, Elmira, New York.

What happened to them?

Younger brother Frank Burnett married Alise and had five daughters including one named Ida, and three sons. They lived in Watkins Glen, New York.

Older brother Henry Burnett went west, then made his way back to Hector, New York. He married Lucia and had two daughters and three sons.

Younger brother Earnest Emeril Burnett died in 1884 at the age of 10.

Younger brother Wallace Pomeroy Burnett married Julia and lived in Horseheads, New York. He died in 1923.

Older sister Mary [Mate] and her husband Frank Stillwell lived in Elmira, New York with their two children.

Older sister Carrie married Frank Bunn and lived in Watkins Glen, New York with their two children.

Younger sister Ada Burnett died in Red Hook, New York in 1959.

Afterward

Ida Burnett married Ziba Baldwin two years and a week after the last account in this diary was written. Ziba was a boatman in Watkins Glen. They had two children - Jennie and Samuel. Ziba died in 1924. Ida died in 1953 at the age of 88. They are buried side by side in Glenwood Cemetery in Watkins Glen, New York.

Ida Burnett Baldwin is buried in Glenwood Cemetery in Watkins Glen between her husband and son.

More Publications from NYHR's
Learning from History series

A Darned Good Time (1868)
by Miss Lucy Potter

My Story - A Year in the Life of a Country Boy 1876
by Earll K. Gurnee

www.NewYorkHistoryReview.com

www.ingramcontent.com/pod-product-compliance
Lightning Source LLC
Chambersburg PA
CBHW051713040426
42446CB00008B/866